The Transformative Influence of Adobe on Technology and Creativity

In the rapidly evolving landscape of technology, few companies have left as indelible a mark as Adobe Systems Incorporated.

Established in 1982 by John Warnock and Charles Geschke, Adobe's journey from its humble beginnings to its current status as a global technology powerhouse is a testament to its innovative spirit and enduring influence.

Through a combination of visionary leadership, groundbreaking software, and a commitment to empowering creativity, Adobe has fundamentally reshaped the way we interact with technology and express our ideas.

Pioneering Creative Tools

One of Adobe's most significant contributions to technology lies in its creation of tools that have become synonymous with digital creativity.

Adobe Photoshop, launched in 1988, revolutionized the way images are edited and manipulated, establishing Adobe's dominance in the graphic design and photography industries.

This transformative software, with its intuitive interface and powerful capabilities, not only revolutionized design processes but also paved the way for digital artistry.

Following the success of Photoshop, Adobe continued its trajectory of innovation with the launch of Adobe Illustrator (1987) and Adobe InDesign (1999).

These tools, respectively, redefined vector-based graphic design and desktop publishing.

The suite of Creative Cloud applications, which now encompasses a wide range of software from video editing (Premiere Pro) to web design (Dreamweaver), has provided professionals and enthusiasts alike with a comprehensive arsenal of tools to bring their creative visions to life.

Standard-Bearers for Digital Document Processing

Adobe's influence is not confined to the realm of creative design alone. The company's development of the Portable Document Format (PDF) in 1993 was a watershed moment in the world of digital documents.

The PDF, initially designed as a platform-independent format for sharing electronic documents, rapidly became the industry standard for distributing information.

Its universal compatibility and ability to retain document formatting across various platforms have made it an essential tool for everything from legal contracts to academic research papers. In 2005, Adobe introduced Adobe Acrobat, which expanded the capabilities of PDFs to include interactive elements, multimedia integration, and electronic forms. This evolution solidified Adobe's position as a leader in document processing technology, enhancing collaboration and communication across industries.

Embracing Digital Transformation

Adobe's influence extends beyond the boundaries of software development. The company has demonstrated a keen understanding of the evolving digital landscape and the need for businesses to adapt to new paradigms.

Adobe's transition from selling boxed software to a subscription-based model with Adobe Creative Cloud was a visionary move that aligned with the shift towards cloud-based services and recurring revenue models.

Furthermore, Adobe has actively championed the cause of digital transformation through its Adobe Document Cloud and Adobe Sign services.

These platforms enable organizations to streamline their workflows, eliminate paper-based processes, and embrace a more efficient and eco-friendly way of conducting business.

Fostering Creative Communities

Adobe's influence on technology goes beyond the mere provision of software tools; it extends to the cultivation of creative communities.

The company has nurtured a vibrant ecosystem of designers, photographers, videographers, and artists who use Adobe products to shape the visual culture of the digital age.

This community has been further empowered through initiatives like Adobe Behance, a platform for sharing and discovering creative work, and Adobe Stock, a marketplace for stock photos, videos, and other assets. Adobe's annual creative conference, Adobe MAX, serves as a hub for creative professionals to gather, learn about new technologies, and gain insights from industry leaders.

This event not only showcases Adobe's latest innovations but also fosters a sense of belonging and shared purpose among creatives.

<u>Pushing Technological Boundaries</u>

Adobe's influence on technology can also be seen in its commitment to pushing the boundaries of what is possible.

The company's research initiatives have led to advancements in areas like artificial intelligence (AI) and machine learning (ML). Adobe Sensei, the company's AI and ML platform, powers features such as content-aware fill in Photoshop and intelligent search in Adobe Stock.

These developments underscore Adobe's dedication to harnessing cutting-edge technology to enhance user experiences and streamline creative workflows.

In the tapestry of technological advancement, Adobe stands as a thread of innovation that has woven itself into every corner of creative expression and digital transformation. From the inception of pioneering design software to the development of industry-standard document formats, Adobe's influence has shaped the way we interact with technology and how we communicate our ideas.

Through a combination of visionary leadership, commitment to creativity, and a deep understanding of the evolving digital landscape, Adobe continues to leave an indelible mark on the realms of technology and creativity.

As we move forward, it is certain that Adobe will remain at the forefront of innovation, driving progress and enabling individuals and businesses to realize their creative potential in the digital age. Thank you John for your amazing work.

Below is space for your notes:

_____

_____

_____

_____

_____

_____

_____

_____

_____

_____

_____

_____

www.ingramcontent.com/pod-product-compliance
Lightning Source LLC
LaVergne TN
LVHW051753050326
832903LV00029B/2880